# VOICE-OVER

POETRY BY ELAINE EQUI

*Friendship with Things,* 1998
*Decoy,* 1994
*Surface Tension,* 1989
*Views without Rooms,* 1989
*Accessories,* 1988
*The Corners of the Mouth,* 1986
*Shrewcrazy,* 1981
*Federal Woman,* 1978

# VOICE-OVER

POEMS BY ELAINE EQUI

COFFEE HOUSE PRESS :: MINNEAPOLIS

Some of these poems have appeared in: *The American Poetry Review, Bathos, Bombay Gin, Caliban, The Columbia Poetry Review, Conjunctions, Cover Art, Gargoyle, Graffiti Rag, Grand Street, Lingo, Long News: in the Short Century, New American Writing, Object, Phoebe, The Plum Review, Promethean, Sugar Mule, Volt, Whatever,* and *The World.*

Coffee House Press is supported in part by a grant provided by the Minnesota State Arts Board, through an appropriation by the Minnesota State Legislature, and in part by a grant from the National Endowment for the Arts. Significant support has also been provided by The McKnight Foundation; Lannan Foundation; Jerome Foundation; Target Stores, Dayton's, and Mervyn's by the Dayton Hudson Foundation; General Mills Foundation; St. Paul Companies; Butler Family Foundation; Honeywell Foundation; Star Tribune Foundation; James R. Thorpe Foundation; Dain Bosworth Foundation; Pentair, Inc.; the Helen L. Kuehn Fund of The Minneapolis Foundation; the law firm of Schwegman, Lundberg, Woessner & Kluth, P.A.; and many individual donors. To you and our many readers across the country, we send our thanks for your continuing support.

Coffee House Press books are available to the trade through our primary distributor, Consortium Book Sales & Distribution, 1045 Westgate Drive, Saint Paul, MN 55114. For personal orders, catalogs, or other information, write to: Coffee House Press, 27 North Fourth Street, Suite 400, Minneapolis, MN 55401.

LIBRARY OF CONGRESS CIP INFORMATION
Equi, Elaine.
    Voice-over : poems / by Elaine Equi.
        p.    cm.
    ISBN 1-56689-078-0 (ALK. PAPER)
    I. Title.
PS3555.Q5V65        1999
811'.54—dc21                                                                98-21159
                                                                                 CIP

10    9    8    7    6    5    4    3    2    1

*printed in Canada*

# CONTENTS

## PART I

## PART II

## PART III

## PART IV

## NOTES

*To My Mother*

". . . the world does not exist in a neutral and impersonal language (it is not, after all, out of a dictionary that the speaker gets his words!), but rather it exists in other people's mouths, in other people's contexts, serving other people's intentions: it is from there that one must take the word and make it one's own."

—M.M. Bakhtin

# PART I

# SPIRIT PHOTOGRAPHY

Where *do* we reside—

in our beer commercials
or somewhere outside of them?

Culture's mirrors
are all one way,

but if the soul
were photographed
would it really be
so predictably vague
and out of focus?

Look, there is the ghost
of a hand,

a family of shadows
stepping out of the sea.

Romantics—

where there is only smoke
we all find someone we know.

Yet the clearly visible
is more mysterious by far.

Our own breasts, arms,
legs, mouths—

unrecognizable
bodies

we can no longer see.

# DETAIL

Not the mansion
but the gate.

Not the cloth
but the crease.

Not the face
but the nose.

Not the speech
but the tone.

Not the pomegranate
but the seeds.

Not the nest
but the egg.

Not Ophelia
but her bouquet.

Not the torso
but the arm.

Not the ship
but its sail.

Not Courbet
but his dog.

Not all of Kerouac
but certainly parts.

Not *Madame Bovary*
as a whole

but as a collection
of individual details

textures, perfumes
that the mind carries off

one at a time.
And always, always

there is the eye
separating, isolating,

calculating difference
like profit and loss.

# SELF PORTRAIT AS YOU

Always receding
you are
what I come out
to see.

You
    "multi-you"

who shuffles the cards,
who never comes forward
but simply appears

on a roller coaster
or looking at the waves—

the static poses
in which I multiply myself.
In a sense you are
what happens to me,

speaking through events
or when you choose

through aura's last residue
of touch—

the product that says "buy me,"
the object that glows.

When I understand
I see

and when I am tired
or confused, I have
nothing to show

that sliver of the whole
that is just you being you—

a new moon which grows the old
again and again, but different
each time. Tonight's heavy as
an enormous peach

drooping over a side street.
The light a fragrant slant
that lingers through next day

changing
as you yourself shift

from lover
to father or mother,

from singer
to silence,
then back to song.

In you
I view myself
at a distance

yet from there
you always seem
more real than me

more able to move
or think or speak

while I can only
write you off,

dreaming of a conversation
where voices don't match faces—
Heidegger's words
in Marilyn Monroe's mouth.

Today seventy percent
of the population believes
in angels, but I don't think
of you in such sentimental terms,

except at times
you seem like a woman,
at times a man.

Impossible to determine
sex, age, race, height—

the answer enfolded,
enveloped somewhere out there
in the head-over-heels blue.

What is the sky anyway,
but a reply to the earth.

# THE LOST LANGUAGE

How and where shall we begin to
recover it? With its pyramids and
vignettes, its keyholes shrouded
in purple fog. This languge which
is made entirely of rumors, echoes,
cadence—without words but perfectly
intelligible. One does not speak,
but is instead immersed in it as one
is said to be immersed in a book
or the weather on an island where
there is only one restaurant, without
any tables or chairs, and with only
two customers. A man and a woman,
both standing: she reading and he
looking out at the sea.

# PINK SHUTTERS

*—for David Trinidad*


Pink Shutters—Pink Shutters!
Sixty-three pairs opened wide
in the narrow alley

as if Mao had once again proclaimed
"Let a hundred windows bloom"
—kiss by kiss.

Shocking Pink! Pagan Pink!
Milk of Magnesia and Panther Pink
seductively pulling us into the air

like a harem of wings
in which we desire and are perhaps afraid
to be lost forever.

We who have just left jobs,
families, packages below
while the eye continues to climb—

refuses, in fact, to come down from
this giddy Jacob's Ladder of Wild Pinks,
Wild Pinks ascending!

# THE HEROINE

has auburn hair
in one chapter
blonde in the next
but remains unchanged
even after discovering
some secret
terrible as a corpse
while looking up
at the oriole
or down the stairs
she has no one to tell
but the blank page
wears a ribbon
seethes with sex
during many
unremarkable encounters
she is not afraid of death
why should she be
at her age
especially when there is
usually a reporter around
to play the cynic
or offer a stick of gum
during tense moments
in which she becomes
aware of her identity
and how it involves choice
sometimes between two men
or a man and a career
or in more modern novels
between a woman and a man

or even two women
between telling and not telling
the strange clues tremble
like leaves badly glued
to a branch later on
we shall read

Dear Miss,
    Now that order has been
restored. Let me say that I
for one never doubted how
like Persephone all grown up
you would be the agent to
bring spring about again,
albeit a bit late and in
autumn. Nevertheless I believe
your father would be proud.
                    Sincerely,
                    A Friend


the end is of course predictable
whatever the choice
we always knew
she would make the right one
before vanishing into
the tapestry of social order
but it's how we see her
in the middle of things
as yet undecided
and standing
so agitated and confused
hair wild
eyes wilder

her will
still virginal
it's like this
that we remember
and like to love her best

# THESIS SENTENCE

Elaine moves a step forward
and everyone else goes back to work.

All day the curtains are moved by the breeze
and some say it is a sign from God.

x writes as if she were God
and knows what it's like to be God all the time.

Others say God is a set of words
held tightly together by an invisible bond—

not one can be added or removed.
The poem is a small machine made of God.

## BEAUTY SECRET

The beautiful
and the hideous

often conspire
in an empire
of appearance.

So which side
would you rather be on—

or NEITHER

like the one
hurrying by,
eyes averted,

arms full of packages:

"These are necessities,
*not* beauty aids.

Excuse me and
thank you very much."

\*

It must be
like losing your
fear of death

to just stop
worrying about
what you look like—

no longer tied
to the lamppost

like a dog
in the rain.

*


From my mother
I learned to fear beauty
the lack of it

and from my father
to distrust it.

Like eyes,

the heart too
turns away

sets its sights
elsewhere.

*

If only people aspired
to the charm
of odd things:

miniature golf courses
or buildings
in a certain light

but, of course,
they don't.

\*

The sun sets.
The vase rests
in the center
of the poem.

It is all
a matter of arrangement.

Relationships
of power

made to seem
natural
and right.

# MONOLOGUE: FRANK O'HARA

Untie your muse
for an hour and stay with me.

I come in pieces
across a great test pattern

or maybe it's what I used to call sky.
The music is certainly blue enough

but not without its own tenderness
like an arrow shot I know not where.

When will you see me as I am
as industrious with grief as you are

clever at hiding your tiredness.
In poems we shine,

and though we say them with conviction,
the words are never really ours for keeps.

# PART II

## CLASS REUNION

In a dream I teach
in a school by a slaughterhouse

children who can hardly stay awake.
Some do nothing but stare at the clock,

while others scribble, determined to mask
with flowery phrases the smell of blood.

My way of doing things, my words
have never been so ineffectual.

Next door is everything we cherish—
enough death to make a person drunk.

The hogs placid, the mood almost pastoral.
The workers joking—old friends,

some I went to school with.
One who always wore a cape,

and one who drove his father's hearse.
"Stay," they say. "Have a drink with us."

# TABLE OF CONTENTS
# FOR AN IMAGINARY BOOK

Spree
Monster Gardens
Up Close, Out Back, Down Under
Flying Backward
The Drunken Voluptuary Workers in the Solarium
Dove Sighting
All The Yellow in the World
A Curse I Put on Myself
Three Sides of the Same Coin
Aria
Night Cream
Good Luck With Your Chaos
The Glass Stagecoach
In the Country of Mauve
Parrots and Dictators
Slumming
Walking the Evening Back Home
A Twelve Course Dinner of Regret
The Gap Gatherer
Burning Down the Ocean
Multiple Choice

# TOTEM

From the
beginning
you wobbled
as if
made dizzy
by your own
height
and I
tethered
at the end
of a long string
would pass
eyes lowered
respectfully
or hurry by
a frightened blur
afraid to
fully grasp
the naked power
of your
tragic gaze
never knowing
or perhaps
always knowing
it is *I*
who protects *you*
from dark
incomprehensible forces
not to your liking
but even more so
from light.

# CAKE, HAT, PILLOW
### —for Joseph Cornell

Some days I wake up so sad,
"morbid" you would say,
and not at all grateful
for the little things
heaped up in the windows
of antique stores that are
mostly overpriced. But then
slowly, especially after
a cappuccino, I feel better,
well enough anyway to stop
at The Photography Store
on Mercer and browse through
the postcards where I find
a 3-D one of Atlantic City
for Rae whose mother is ill
and an apocalyptic one for myself
of a small girl carrying a satchel
down an empty road. The sky behind
her is almost green. The clouds
ominous, like a cross between
Revelations and *The Wizard of Oz.*
There is a story there, but probably
not one that I will read or write today.
Today my ambitions are smaller
and fit neatly on the back
of this third card, picked out
just for you Joseph Cornell.
On it are three images in a row:
a white cake next to a white hat
next to a white pillow. Remember,

you said you only wanted "white magic."
Or maybe it reminds me of how
sometimes while working on your boxes,
you would also bake cakes, staying up
until dawn, then falling asleep in
one of the kitchen's straight-backed chairs.
I don't know if you ever wore or would
want a fedora. But a pillow—considering
the vicissitude of even the mildest,
most pleasant, most temperate of lives
(yours, mine)—who would not like a pillow?

# BARTLETT'S QUOTATIONS

Here are half a dozen leaves,
city leaves, weighed down under
centuries of pronouncements
which were gathered by someone who,
like any good Victorian housewife,
decided what should be thrown out
and what saved. Coherent and neat
as my desire to quote from a
particular sunny day when nothing
in particular happened. Forgotten
for years, until I come upon them
again in the middle of winter.
Now, stiff as paper fans, some are
the color of tea, and some of mud
and some are a mottled russet and gold.
Startling. Autumn-hearted, ash-hearted.
Each leaf like a flame, like a bit
of fire held in the hand.

# SECOND THOUGHTS

*—for Rae Armantrout*

1. Once one has learned the trick of keeping up appearances—
   it's very hard to get beyond that.


2. To vegetate: from the Latin *vegetare* meaning to enliven.


3. Androgynous-looking men and women always look androgynous
   in the same way—as if there were a right and wrong way to do it.


4. Speaking a language is different from feeling it. One Japanese
   woman I know says that when she swears in English, she feels
   nothing.


5. Doesn't it seem wonderfully optimistic when someone you hardly
   know signs a note "Love"? And, in fact, doesn't it make you love
   them just a little for doing it?


6. The light shines on the lavender, but the effect is one of their
   being illuminated from within—as if the external light only drew
   our attention to the inner light that is theirs alone.


7. Bedded down like a mollusk.

8. Unlikely heroes: Fate in the musical comedies of the 50s. Time in the new novel of the 60s. Language in the critical thinking of the 70s.

9. Where would I like to die? In a bakery, I think—as in one of those religions where the corpse is surrounded by sweets and fruit.

10. Not every stone that's been rejected by the builder can become the cornerstone—just one of them.

11. The sunflowers are the table's antennae.

12. There are women who begin cleaning, then discover that they can't stop. It's the housewife's version of *The Red Shoes* and it really does happen.

13. My greed is never so apparent as when I pray—yet isn't it also a sign of faith?

14. Like any relationship, a new sex fantasy needs to be carefully cultivated. Some you may entertain only briefly, but others can last a lifetime.

15. Sexual fantasies are more than just mood music.

16. Her objects were arranged on the shelf like a sentence beginning with an Aztec sacrificial knife and ending with the photograph of an old woman.

17. My father had a genius for appreciating kitsch, and his talent always made me feel there were depths I would never be able to sink to.

18. On being moved by a will other than one's own: she said her journal was living her life for her; she said she had begun to feel like she was her cat's pet!

19. What speech shares with birds: both live in the air.

20. Confidence comes from knowing you can always get back what you lose.

21. Messiah Complex: One at a time, imagine everyone you know as dead; then, one at a time, bring them back to life again.

22. What It Amounts To: One particularly vivid childhood memory I have is of literally standing on a hill of beans. A six or seven foot hill—which given the neighborhood I grew up in seems highly unlikely. Nevertheless . . .

23. To muse: from the Latin *mus* meaning snout!

24. To be understood, cliches are as necessary as syntax or grammar.

25. Every day I discover more and more products I can't live without.

26. Do men find themselves talking in a voice that is not quite their own—slightly higher, lower, younger—as often as women do?

27. All voices have a tactile quality and are meant to be felt as well as heard.

28. There are people who look out the window to see the future—its arrival.

29. Even a landscape can make a gesture toward us.

# (an) OBJECT

shining
in the cold

while memory
completes
its drawing

# SIGN

A
big
red
flashing
arrow

directs
us
behind
the
dark
mysterious
curtain

where
ghosts
of
steam
and
suds
emerge

And
though
it
is
only
a
car wash

I
come
away
thinking
that
this
is
what
we
need
in
life

more
arrows

## NOT SO FAST

Jakob Boehme stands
on the top rung
of Jacob's Ladder.
It does not lean
against anything.
Clouds rush between
his outstretched hands.
He cannot see God
but he can see
Adam Kadmon, the giant
without a face,
the face wiped clean
of features—nothing
but a lightbulb
between two ears.
And yet he seems
to be smiling
especially when
an angry woman
climbs up after Boehme,
grabs him by the leg
and shouts: "Hold on!
Before *you* go off to heaven,
*I'd* like a word with you."

# ARMANI WEATHER

In that long
navy blue
cashmere coat,
he was made
to do nothing
but lean against
tall buildings.
A somber
exclamation point,
eating an apple—
turning it slowly
into ballet.
How extravagant
yet restrained,
the way he wears
the space
around his body
loosely.
Even the light matches,
pale and cold
and slightly green,
like the apple
against his dark skin.

# REMORSE AFTER SHOPPING

Why did I buy it?
What was I thinking?
It's all wrong.
Tacky, but not in a good way.
It looks suburban.
It spells housewife.
Too nurturing.
I don't even have kids.
No one will take me seriously.
It must have been the lighting.
I was in a hurry.
I don't even want to return it.
Just get it out of here.
Throw it away.

# SOMEONE IS TRYING TO CALL

I see
a rainy man
on a bald day.

He doesn't have change

and you're so busy
making yourself nervous

you wouldn't hear
an avalanche of rose petals
if they fell on you.

# DESIRE IN WINTER

With your white
that is almost blue.

With your blue
that is almost gray.

With your gray
that is almost white.

Again you come
wrapped in the coldness

of a cloud, a drifter
with edges that are not distinct.

This is our nostalgia
for what we have always wanted

and what has never been.
You know.

You carry our secrets
within you. You carry them away

to places beyond
that will one day seem familiar.

# SHIELD

*—for Amy Gerstler*


What belongs to one
cannot belong to another.

The name and the property
protected by its totem
(insignias and emblems).

A crest bulging above a door
(dolphin and rose).

And yet there are things
we have in common
(ideas written in the blue
diary of the sky).

Nomadic animals that travel
from land to land.

I pick up your book
and know somehow it is yours.

I put it down
and the sentences mingle with mine

(moving slowly as if in a caravan)

and even on my shield
the gryphon, the lion,
the alligator too
are beginning to move.

# PART III

# WANG WEI'S MOON

*—for David Shapiro*

Leisurely
it comes out—

new moon
like the eyebrow
of a moth,

full moon
that burns
the pines,

or suddenly
                    sad

remote
above a gate,

or glaring
                    clarity

like a lamp
that quiets windows.

Cold
it tumbles into
random shadows

alarming birds,

       far far
stone cliffs
shine

as someone
washes silk
in moonlight.

Unsteady images
tied to whiteness.

Stars
float up
toward dawn.

## ALMOST TRANSPARENT

—*for Lorine Niedecker*


You and your books:

>       quotes
>       fly overhead
>       like clouds

Your words:

>       quick and
>       emerald green

>       chameleon-like
>       in the spic and span
>       kitchen

You think you've disappeared—

Stoic:

>       a Garbo
>       of the Midwest,

>       a swamp queen

>       Ms. Dickinson
>       comes visit
>       Mr. Basho
>       comes for tea

You *think* you're part of the landscape

    soaked-in
    water-voiced

but it's you I see moving (isn't it?)

    behind the sheer
    almost transparent curtain
    of your poems

# CUPBOARD / SHRINE

If I have
an image of mind

it's as
general store:

boxes and
canned goods

to be moved
and dusted behind.

The idea
and its opposite,

paint and turpentine,
side by side—

honey and vinegar
on the shelf below.

## IN MAY

I hear something more
(new?) soar
       in your voice

not a bird
just God-like ranging
       over land

not only digging
but flight too
       creates depth

# FROM LORINE

How am I really?
I'm all right.
I enjoy my home,
even myself sometimes.
Enmeshed in nuisances
of course but no real troubles.
How are you really?

*

Hair almost all gray now?

Eyebrows are the last
to show age and eyes never.

*

The world is busy
rushing past my door . . .

life is weeds
instead of grass—
not even weeds
but water.

*

Don't send Xmas present—

I have something for you
not at all expensive either.

So just draw a picture
of a pine tree

which is one kind of tree
I don't have.

\*

Last night
it rained here. Everything
has decided to live.

Luffly
                    little dellycut moments

strings of geese
going over
                    and spiders
                    starting to crawl.

It has been hard
to sell magic—
will the time come
when it can't
be *given* away?

# FENNEL

What is there to say about fennel—with its heavy
licorice tongue that makes one feel both drowsy and
wide awake? Whole it looks remarkably like a hookah
or else a bottle of eau de cologne. And the taste
is like that too. A sort of cigarette and breath
mint swallowed all in one bite. Cut into, its flesh
unwinds like a roll of film—shot half in winter,
half in spring. As much a liqueur as fruit or
vegetable. As much a beginning as an end.

## STARTING TO RAIN
*—for Joe Brainard*


Distracted, I leave
the therapist's office
but even walking fast
they catch my eye

make me stop
and look

while they look back.

Dark and light
blue pansies
in a white window box.

So small—

how did they manage
to make themselves heard?

# ANOTHER WALL TO WALK THROUGH

Unwanted thoughts
become walls.

The world is diluted.

The walls grow
more thoughtful.

They linger
by placing themselves
before the eye.

A series of screens
imposed or superimposed on,

so that even your bed
is like a hallucination
recognized only by touch
or smell.

Then words are suddenly
far away and you are
no longer the hunter
coming out of the mist.

Your hair is heavy
on your head.

Your head heavy
heaped with hundreds
of unwanted flowers.

They cover the walls
with hesitation

but still it is
a hesitation
that holds in place.

# LETTER OF RECOMMENDATION

Please say something really good,
no, *great* about yourself. I would
but I am watching a porno movie
and have no time to write.
The woman astride the man is a ghost
and the fact that she's dead
makes it seem more artistic.
I'm afraid I'll be busy for months.
You know I love your work,
think highly of you—
but then these ghosts arrive
and somehow a person can't say no.
They are so demanding.
To get away even for coffee
seems a lot. It's difficult
to know where it will end,
especially when he doesn't suspect
the ghost is really a brunette actress
in a blonde wig. She says
part of him wants to be fooled.
Meanwhile, remember how brave
and talented you are.
I would add beautiful too
but that might sound strange.
So just write anything,
something glowing—
and sign my name.

# NIGHT SCHOOL

No one knows
what mind is
or how to get there.

It is like
a conversation
that never ends

always more to say,
someone breathing
over the phone

even after
you hang up,
even after they die.

*

Old coats, old vases
that were promised . . .

You think you remember
the way

past the community college
where you never went
to night school,

the stars so pretty
to look at
while driving home.

# PART IV

PART IV

# LITTLE LANDSCAPE

Little landscape
always at breast
equals water
under the bridge.
A flowing past
where faces and events
are not fixed.
The elves in selves
broken and darting,
nerves numbed by wind.
The shadow pours itself
out on the grass.
The dark arches
rise and cross over.

# VOICE-OVER

1.
Climbing the Tower of Babel
we ascend into noise,

every sort of hybrid—
pig squeals grafted onto wheels

burning rubber.
But coming down, dissonance fades

and contradictions fold
into a single voice.

Reassuringly direct, it says:
"Psychic advisors are waiting."

It says: "Perfection is coming."
It says: "Call now for free samples."

It says: "Week after week, we tackle
the questions you'd like to ask God."


2.
Once upon a time,
far away, in a booth
of glass and light

a man cleared his throat
and a woman adjusted her headphones
in order to send their breath—

just the sound of it—

like bees
to circle and inflate
all things hollow,

sculpting the air itself
into a story
we soon came to think of as ours.

This narrow world,
a silent movie,
longs for those voices

on high to float down
with their sprigs of color,
canned laughter,
their rational explanations
lovingly applied.


3.
Disembodied
the voice
conveys
intimacy
(even personality)
but at a distance.
Thus we are
less judgmental,
more willing
to listen
and eager to buy.

In poetry too
we like our lyricism
minus the garlic
on the poet's breath.


4.
Here is stock footage of clouds
followed by mudslides, earthquakes, monsoons—

a time-lapse change of seasons
over which the narrator says:
"We've come through it all and so can you."

Don't worry.
Here is a gloved hand, a pair of scissors,
a paper heart.

Don't worry.
"Make yourself in as passive,
or receptive a state of mind as you can."

(Almost as if you were taking dictation.)
"Put your trust in the inexhaustible
nature of the murmur."

Don't worry.
Voice imposes order. From above.
Someone else's voice.

Using violence first and then seduction
or vice-versa.

The mother's and then the father's voice.
The neutral voice of science
familiar as a lullaby.


5.
How like
an ear
the earth

listens,
lies down
to listen—

a spoonful
of sounds
dissolving

in the dream
where mouths move
out of sync.


6.
Scripted,
it is not natural.

It only appears that way
to sell the Grecian urn
or Grecian Formula 44—

the death in the family
like a used car.

And yet
we do hear them,

these voices.

Like St. Joan
have grown used to them.

Inside and out.

Diaphanous as scarves.
Drawn closer.

Sometimes, we even answer.
Glad we're not alone.

# KARAOKE POEM

All day
I mouth the fantasies
of someone else.

I see it
and say it.

Ask for a tall cold one,
a red hot one.

Ask for the hunky guy
on the calendar
splayed over a rock.

All day
I move like a woman
possessed.

Move my hips
to get into a groove.

My hands
like a nervous Judy Garland
shooing flies.

In my prep school drag,
in my bondage and discipline
drag,

how long,
how long have I waited

for that moment
(there are only a few)

when I could turn

like a record,
like Sinatra—

my coat draped
over my shoulder—

when I could turn
and walk away.

# HINGE

Nothing needs us
but we need
a lot of reassurance
before we can reassure
those things we thought
we needed that they exist too.
Making room for them
is like making a room for them.
That's why often we draw doors
on what we want, and after
a while, add windows too.
We love our sky.
We love our blueprints.
Their reassuring color
that gives a feeling of similarity
where one does not necessarily exist.

# REVELATION
*—for Charles Simic*

The man on the corner
who always talked to himself
about the end of the world

now has a cellular phone
and discusses with a similar man
on another corner
signs visible only to them.

When they finish
each will phone two others
who in turn will phone two more.

"Tonight," they mumble,
"at 7:15 or 8:00."

Meanwhile we hurry by
oblivious to the dark cloud
spreading its one good wing,

the traffic cop riding his pale horse.

# LIKE ROBINSON CRUSOE

I too live on an island
with a man I met on a Friday.
And I too have a Bible,
a table, a saucepan, a pen
with which to write in my journal.
The world, though all around,
seems far away. Gone—even as
we preserve its rituals, its order,
try to create again and again
whatever once was meant by it, them.

# GOLD SANDALS

*—for Ann Lauterbach*

Theatrical
as a shepherd of air
who is followed
by music
rather than sheep.
They always know
where to go next.
Trailblazers
that light the way.
A firewalk to
the grocery store.
A cakewalk home
with the horrible
Aztec gold of summer.
Slip-shod, gilded.
As if I had become
this horrible
but fascinating person.
Me—in my
alchemist slippers.
Me with my miser ways.

# EDWARD HOPPER

His figures lean
like plants
toward light.

Transfixed—

they bring
a smile
to our lips

as if this was
the last time
we'd seen ourselves
naked,

the way
a stranger might,
in passing.

The body itself
a lamp
in a drab room

standing
on the threshold
of something big.

This sense of eternity
however brief—

O sidelong glance
in whose indifference
I bask,

years from now
is it this
you will return to me?

# THE ORIGAMI OF TIME
—*for Martine Bellen*


O how I love clocks,
                their roundness.

*Mother Time*—

a drop of bright blood
enclosed in quartz
(cameo-like).

*

Behind their plain faces
one senses complexity.

Bewitching
in its folds
and creases.

Children play
near the edge.

Doves leap
from its high places.

## JEROME MEDITATING

The eyes are closed.
The windows are open.
The blue towel is spread
in the center of the floor.

The windows are open.
The legs are crossed
in the center of the floor.
Shirtless. Shoeless.

The legs are crossed.
The chest is bare.
Shirtless. Shoeless,
with a hole in your left sock.

The chest is bare.
The skin pale.
With a hole in your left sock,
you count from one to ten.

The skin pale.
The breath steady.
You count from one to ten
like a child practicing scales.

The breath steady
in spite of thoughts that dart and swoop
like a child practicing scales
during rush hour.

In spite of thoughts that dart and swoop,
a single melody heard
during rush hour—
somewhere someone whistling an unfamiliar tune.

A single melody heard
comprised of all the noise, horns, and birds.
Somewhere someone whistling an unfamiliar tune.
Then intermittent moments of calm.

Comprised of all the noise, horns, and birds,
discreetly a breeze enters the room.
Then intermittent moments of calm.
Hands resting on knees.

Discreetly a breeze enters the room
passing like a glance over
hands resting on knees,
books in piles all around.

Passing like a glance over—
what is it you are thinking now?
Books in piles all around:
Walter Benjamin and Meister Eckhart.

What is it you are thinking now,
at this moment, in this room—
Walter Benjamin? Meister Eckhart?
The incense continues to burn.

At this moment, in this room,
there's a vase of pussy willows behind your head.
The incense continues to burn,
but the candles remain unlit.

Yet even with pussy willows behind your head,
you seem sober, so absorbed.
The candles remain unlit
though the room grows dark.

You seem sober, so absorbed,
the stillness filling every corner
as the room grows dark
and I watch as if you were asleep.

The stillness filling every corner,
in the kitchen I put on water for tea
and watch as if you were asleep . . .
nothing but the sound of your heartbeat.

In the kitchen I put on water for tea,
aware of the echo each move makes.
Nothing but the sound of your heartbeat
like a shell bringing the ocean home.

## MINE

I hide it
when even I
can't find it,

wordsmall

it directs
everything—

returns
as a gift
from someone else.

# NOTES

### WANG WEI'S MOON

This cento is composed entirely of many of my favorite lines about moonlight by the T'ang dynasty poet, Wang Wei. All are from wonderful translations done by Tony Barnstone, Willis Barnstone, and Xu Haixin.

### FROM LORINE

This poem is also a collage of lines and phrases (slightly edited) from Lorine Niedecker's letters. Most were written to Louis Zukofsky, although the last line is from a letter to Harriet Monroe, then the editor of *Poetry Magazine*.

### VOICE-OVER

The quotes in section one were compiled from The Psychic Readers Network, The Faith and Values Network, and an ad for Royal Caribbean Cruise Ships. The quotes in section four are from Andre Breton's *Manifestoes of Surrealism*.